Family Business Values:
How to Assure a Legacy of Continuity and Success

Craig E. Aronoff, Ph.D. and
John L. Ward, Ph.D.

Family Business Leadership Series, No. 12

Family Enterprise Publishers
P.O. Box 4356
Marietta, GA 30061-4356
800-551-0633
www.efamilybusiness.com

ISSN: 1071-5010
ISBN: 1-891652-02-8
© 2001
Second Printing

Family Business Leadership Series

We believe that family businesses are special, not only to the families that own and manage them but to our society and to the private enterprise system. Having worked and interacted with hundreds of family enterprises in the past twenty years, we offer the insights of that experience and the collected wisdom of the world's best and most successful family firms.

This volume is a part of a series offering practical guidance for family businesses seeking to manage the special challenges and opportunities confronting them.

To order additional copies, contact:
Family Enterprise Publishers℠
1220-B Kennestone Circle
Post Office Box 4356
Marietta, Georgia 30061-4356
Tel: 800-551-0633
Web Sites: www.efamilybusiness.com

Quantity discounts are available.

Other volumes in the series include:

Family Business Succession: The Final Test of Greatness

Family Meetings: How to Build a Stronger Family and a Stronger Business

Another Kind of Hero: Preparing Successors For Leadership

How Families Work Together

Family Business Compensation

How to Choose & Use Advisors: Getting the Best Professional Family Business Advice

Financing Transitions: Managing Capital and Liquidity in the Family Business

Family Business Governance: Maximizing Family and Business Potential

Preparing Your Family Business For Strategic Change

Making Sibling Teams Work: The Next Generation

Developing Family Business Policies: Your Guide to the Future

More Than Family: Non-Family Executives in the Family Business

Make Change Your Family Business Tradition

Family Business Ownership: How To Be An Effective Shareholder

Contents

Tables and Exhibits

Introduction

Despite all the rhetoric about values these days, relatively few people are prepared to see how values shape our day-to-day lives and fortunes. Values are the cornerstone of human achievement and commitment. They have "life-giving power" to motivate people and lend meaning to work, as nineteenth-century author John Ruskin wrote. **Values inspire people to do things that are difficult, to make commitments that require discipline, to stick to plans for the long haul.** Values are the bedrock of culture in business and in families alike. Culture and values in turn underlie all habits of success in both realms.

Just twenty years ago, the concept of corporate culture was alien to most businesspeople. Today, almost anyone involved in business can apply the term to his or her enterprise. Business leaders understand that the financial success of any company ultimately rests upon its culture and the underlying values. The corporate cultures of the most successful companies have been widely studied and promoted as models.

The most successful families, too, have strong values rooted in members' emotional bonds, blood ties and shared history. Values underpin decision making in every core family function, from child-rearing to estate planning. Ideally, **shared values enable family members to derive pleasure and meaning from sustaining cross-generational relationships and striving toward mutual goals.**

What happens when the values driving a powerful business culture, and the values underpinning a healthy family culture, overlap? **When an owning family's values form the heart of a business's culture, some vital synergies can arise. In fact, an enduring commitment to values is the greatest strength a family can bring to business ownership.**

Shared values also can help overcome the conflicts inherent to family business ownership. When family and business pull apart over time, as they invariably do, families need a compelling rationale to stick together. Values can be the glue that bonds family and business. Values provide satisfying answers to such questions as, Why

Values inspire people to do things that are difficult, to make commitments that require discipline, to stick to plans for the long haul.

1

do we work so hard? Why bother to pass on this business? Why should we make the sacrifices involved in owning and operating a family business? That's why the focus of this booklet, values and values education, is also a common focus among the most successful business-owning families we have seen. The earlier a business leader begins tapping the potential strength of shared values in the family and the business, the better the chances of harmony and success. Perhaps most important, a dynamic, resilient value system is the most enduring living legacy one generation can leave the next.

When an owning family's values form the heart of a business's culture, some vital synergies can arise. In fact, an enduring commitment to values is the greatest strength a family can bring to business ownership.

This booklet is a guide to understanding values and tapping their power in families and in business. It is written for family business leaders and owners intent on realizing the rich synergies shared values can create, on maximizing the unique competitive strengths of family business, and on raising the chances of long-term family business survival. Part I explores the power of values as the bedrock of family business culture, showing in practical terms how values can strengthen day-to-day operations. Part II explains the role of values in resolving the inherent conflicts between family and business. It also describes the unique synergies that can arise in the value systems of healthy families and well-run business. Part III explains several qualities of productive values and describes twenty special values shared by many successful family businesses. Parts IV and V give tips and techniques for identifying, nurturing and passing on values in the family and the business. And Part VI offers help renewing and reinterpreting values so that they retain their productive power in today's fast-changing world.

I. *The Power of Values in the Family Business*

A Seattle salesperson at Nordstrom, the big family-controlled retail chain, had just finished serving a customer when she noticed the woman had left her plane ticket at the counter before racing off to the airport.

The salesperson telephoned the airline and asked a representative to write another ticket for the traveler. When the airline refused, the Nordstrom employee jumped in a cab, rode out to the Seattle-Tacoma airport, found the customer and delivered the ticket herself. Nordstrom later reimbursed her for her cab fare.

Such tales of employee "heroics" adorn the walls of back offices at Nordstrom stores all over the country. As Robert Spector and Patrick McCarthy say in their 1995 book, *The Nordstrom Way: Inside America's No. 1 Customer Service Company,* Nordstrom employees go beyond the call of duty to serve customers every day. Among these "true tales of incredible customer service:" An employee warms up a customer's car in the dead of winter. Another Nordstrom salesperson satisfies a customer by running across the street to a competitor's store to find a pair of slacks that is temporarily sold out at Nordstrom. Yet another employee ships a batch of new shirts to Sweden to please a customer upset over ruining his new Nordstrom shirts in the laundry.

Nordstrom inspires such enviable performance partly by empowering its employees to make decisions and authorizing its managers to live with those decisions. As a result, shopping with a Nordstrom salesperson is like working with the owner of a small business, Spector and McCarthy write, fostering customer service cited by management guru Tom Peters for "matchless quality."

At the heart of those high standards is a core value of the Nordstrom family: Placing faith and trust in their frontline people. "If that confidence in the individual is repeated over and over and over again, it creates power," says co-chairman Bruce Nordstrom. No wonder, as Spector and McCarthy write, "Nordstrom's supreme advantage over its competition is that it has been and will continue to be controlled and operated by the Nordstrom family. Family control brings an institutional memory, a consistent message and stability for long-range planning."

The values of people who own, run and operate businesses play out in powerful ways. Defined as people's most deeply held principles, concerns or moral or ethical goals, values shape behavior. They arise from people's beliefs about such fundamental issues as the nature of man, the future of humanity, the mission of business in society, or people's obligations to each other. **Values tend to endure over time. When shared among owners, decisionmakers and employees in a business, they have great power in shaping the business's performance and results.**

John Kotter and James Heskett found in an 11-year study of more than 200 publicly held companies that those that valued customers, stockholders and employees and fostered leadership by managers at all levels outperformed others by a huge margin. These strong-culture companies increased revenue more than four times faster, created jobs more than seven times faster and grew profit several hundredfold more quickly, as Kotter and Heskett reported in *Corporate Culture and Performance* (Free Press, 1992). As Terrence E. Deal and Allen A. Kennedy said in their book, *The New Corporate Cultures* (Perseus Books, 1999), "If you look closely at any highly respected company, you're bound to find a distinctive culture."

> *Values tend to endure over time. When shared among owners, decision-makers and employees in a business, they have great power in shaping the business's performance and results.*

Family businesses have a special competitive advantage in this regard. Despite the growing attention to corporate culture among leaders of publicly held businesses, Wall Street still uses the word "value" in its singular form. It may refer to a variety of financial indicators, from share price to return on investment or market share, but it usually boils down to one thing: Money. In family business, "values" are used far more often in their plural form. Family business owners have the freedom to recognize a broader reality that reaches beyond financial goals. Family businesses also have the vast potential advantage of a cohesive owning family with shared values.

The power of values plays out in business in at least a dozen major ways. (Please see Table 1.) Let's take a closer look.

THE POWER OF VALUES IN FAMILY BUSINESS

1. Laying the bedrock for corporate culture.
2. Providing a template for decision making.
3. Inspiring top performance.
4. Supporting a patient, long-term view.
5. Reducing the cost of capital.
6. Challenging conventional thinking.
7. Adapting to change.
8. Improving strategic planning.
9. Executing strategy.
10. Forging strategic alliances.
11. Recruiting and retaining employees.
12. Lending meaning to work.

1. Laying the bedrock for corporate culture.

Corporate culture is the buildup of beliefs and values that drive the business, and the day-to-day assumptions and behaviors that reflect those values. As a business grows, the business leader builds a culture by promoting or exemplifying certain values. Culture and values in turn drive decision making in all dimensions of management, from succession to strategic planning.

2. Providing a template for decision making.

Consciously or not, business decisionmakers view all questions through a framework of values. A business owner's reflections on where to invest earnings are shaped by values relating to competitiveness. If staying competitive is a core value, the business leader may decide to open new markets or expand capacity at the expense of other outcomes, such as payback to owners or higher salaries. A business leader doing strategic planning may be guided by the value placed on honesty — a rigorous assessment of the business's strengths and weaknesses in relation to competitors, and a willingness to make tough decisions based on that assessment. A business owner deciding whether to name independent directors to the company's board may be guided by the value he or she places on accountability.

Values also shape a business's response to crisis. When calamity strikes, there's no time to hold a meeting and concoct an orchestrated response. Managers and employees alike must react based on a shared understanding of what's important. James E. Burke's response to crisis at Johnson & Johnson in 1982, when seven people died taking Tylenol Extra-Strength capsules laced with cyanide, is a textbook case. Amid mounting consumer panic, Burke acted quickly to reassure the public and save the Tylenol franchise. He was absolutely honest with the media and devoted his executive team full-time to the crisis. He also took the unprecedented step of removing every bottle of Tylenol from the shelves during the crisis. His actions preserved consumer trust in the Tylenol brand.

> *Consciously or not, business decisionmakers view all questions through a framework of values.*

In interviews, Burke later made it clear that a single value — to "trust people until they prove themselves unworthy of that trust" — underpinned all his actions. That value was rooted in his own family upbringing. It also was a pillar of Johnson & Johnson's corporate culture, he told an interviewer for *Management Review* in 1996. "I was lucky. I had a family who thought the same way. The company I went to work for thought the same way," Burke said. The value of trust was a theme running through Burke's life and leadership.

3. Inspiring top performance.

Values are powerful motivators of people. Bottom-line objectives typically fall short in building a vision for the future. Quarterly profit targets don't stimulate most people for long. Business leaders who place great faith in financial incentives are often disappointed. "I put in a dental plan, but I don't see any increase in productivity," the business leader may lament. **Organizations that achieve lasting competitive advantage typically find some higher motivation that enables participants to feel pride in the organization and to believe in what they're doing.** These business owners, managers and employees in turn tend to approach the business with enthusiasm and insights that fuel new strategies.

> *Values are powerful motivators of people.*

We know food-processing and newspaper-publishing businesses whose owners believe their businesses make a special contribution to society. The family owners of one scrap dealer see themselves as recyclers, helping the environment. In *Built to Last: Successful Habits of Visionary Companies* (New York: Harper-Business, 1994), authors James Collins and Jerry Porras wrote, "Visionary companies pursue a cluster of objectives, of which making money is only one ... They're guided by a core ideology — core values and sense of purpose beyond just making money."

As values come to life in a business culture, they take on a self-renewing energy. People who are drawn to work in a business typically share its values; so do people who are promoted to leadership positions. That is a powerful source of efficiency. If a business has the right values for success, it tends to employ and attract people who will achieve it.

4. Supporting a patient, long-term view.

A vision that transcends quarterly profit can strengthen owners' resolve and help them stay the course through economic and political upheaval. Johnstons of Elgin, a fine woolens producer based in Elgin, Morayshire, Scotland, survived and prospered through seven generations of ownership by two families by adhering to core values of fine craftsmanship, superb quality, a swiftness to embrace the newest technology and raw materials, and a global outlook in seeking both raw materials and products. Using fine fibers such as Scottish woolens, Chinese cashmere and South American vicuna, the company continually created soft, luxurious new fabrics and garments for global markets, building a well-known and respected brand name.

Organizations that achieve lasting competitive advantage typically find some higher motivation that enables participants to feel pride in the organization and to believe in what they're doing.

During Johnstons' two centuries of survival and success, sweeping changes in finance, transportation, communication, business practices and fashion occurred. Sources of power shifted from water to steam to gas to electricity. Transportation evolved from sailing ships and horse to railroads, trucks and airfreight. The Suez and Panama Canals opened, remaking global trade routes. Revenue and raw material supplies to the business waxed and waned as governments rose and fell and economies soared and crashed. The company learned to manage large inventories to guard against supply interruptions and to cope with a Pandora's box of other risks associated with import-export trade. Johnstons changed anything and everything to adapt and survive through the generations except core values and competencies. Through it all, the owning families took a long-term view, understanding that Johnstons' fundamental principles of doing business would enable the company to continue to create value in world markets.

5. Reducing the cost of capital.

Shared values among owners can have the effect of reducing a business's cost of capital by fostering shareholder solidarity, commitment and enthusiasm. Shareholders who have a reason to stick together are more likely to support appropriate risk-taking, to sacrifice short-term liquidity for long-term business goals and to refrain from draining capital from the business for personal needs. All this enables the business to build on a relatively low-cost capital base and reduce need for debt, selling stock to the public or taking on partners who may not share family members' long-term view.

As values come to life in a business culture, they take on a self-renewing energy. People who are drawn to work in a business typically share its values; so do people who are promoted to leadership positions. That is a powerful source of efficiency. If a business has the right values for success, it tends to employ and attract people who will achieve it.

6. Challenging conventional thinking.

Because values don't originate in the marketplace, but in human beliefs and experience, they often require business owners to challenge common assumptions about how business is done. The results can be surprisingly good. The third generation owners of one big food-products company stand on principle in idling their nationwide operations every Sabbath, including several factories and a large fleet of trucks. They also stress stewardship, place a high value on respecting employees, and tithe to their church as a business and as individuals. In an outcome that would no doubt surprise competitors, their company's returns still match and often exceed the competition's.

This family achieves all that partly by adhering to a principle of providing value to the customer. The company prices its products well below the next biggest national brand. Its ability to do that springs from two values laid down by the founder. The first, "find a better way," has driven the family to develop new technology and other operating innovations that hold down costs. The founder's second maxim, "double it," has motivated the family to make the sacrifices necessary to double sales volume every four years.

Another family business, Chick-fil-A, owned by Atlanta's Cathy family, closes its operations every Sunday, including 800 fast-food restaurant outlets. As a result, a family executive says, its employees are fresher when they return to work Monday after a day of rest. That reduces costly attrition; "We have one of the lowest rates of turnover in the industry," a family executive says.

Shared values among owners can have the effect of reducing a business's cost of capital by fostering shareholder solidarity, commitment and enthusiasm. Shareholders who have a reason to stick together are more likely to support appropriate risk-taking, to sacrifice short-term liquidity for long-term business goals and to refrain from draining capital from the business for personal needs.

7. Adapting to change.

Values can give business leaders and owners the courage to take steps in new, ambiguous directions. *Built to Last* calls this kind of adaptation "evolutionary progress." At Warren Featherbone Co., seven fundamental values, including creative thinking and "maximizing the company's ability to adapt," are the platform upon which the company has adapted through over a century of changing markets, says fourth-generation family leader Charles E. "Gus" Whalen. Founded in 1883 in Three Oaks, MI, as a maker of corset stiffeners, Warren Featherbone faltered in the 1930s when plastics supplanted its basic material, split turkey quills. But the company embraced the juggernaut that threatened to destroy it and fielded a new product, plastic baby pants, and a line of plastic apparel.

Heavy competition and deteriorating labor relations again weakened Featherbone after World War II. It acquired an infantwear maker and relocated to Gainesville, GA, in 1957. By 1966 the company began a steady recovery in sales and profit based upon baby pants and mid-priced infant wear. Once again in the mid-1970s, a powerhouse consumer product — the disposable diaper — ravaged its markets. Again, Warren Featherbone embraced change, developing fancy disposable diaper cover-ups that grew into a new line of toddler wear. Today the company continues to compete successfully with low-cost off-shore apparel manufacturers partly through a "quick response" program, using technology to cement operating alliances with suppliers and retailers.

8. Improving strategic planning.

Core values can help business leaders avoid bogging down in past successes and lift their eyes to the horizon. That perspective lends balance and breadth to strategic decision making. The authors of *Built to Last* point out that enduring companies apply three tests in deciding what products and services to offer: What you stand for; What you're good at; What people will pay you for. (*Inc.*, October 1997). When a company's identity can't be separated from a few key products — any of which may become obsolete — or from the identity of its leader, it can't be known for what it stands for. Nor can it endure in any meaningful form.

Core values can help business leaders avoid bogging down in past successes and lift their eyes to the horizon. That perspective lends balance and breadth to strategic decision making.

J. Smith Lanier, named 1998 Small Business Person of the Year by the Small Business Council of America, is the septuagenarian patriarch of two century-old family businesses. One of them, ITC Holding Co., is an independent telephone company in West Point, GA, that transformed itself from a local monopoly into a strong player in telecommunications, right from the starting block of industry deregulation in the 1980s. While some competitors sat back and allowed themselves to be swallowed up in the newly competitive environment, Lanier family managers, guided by the shared values of stewardship and embracing change, capitalized quickly on new opportunities.

Executives "started picking up niche markets that they thought would be good," Mr. Lanier recalls. They made some good picks. Resale of long-distance telephone service was an initial venture. "Then they came up with the little idea of a voice mailbox," Mr. Lanier recalls in an interview. Back then, voicemail was a novelty, and ITC was the only independent telephone company in the nation that offered it. The huge

When strategy is a good fit with owners', managers' and employees' values, it is likely to be implemented with greater energy, enthusiasm and insight. Bringing values to life imparts passion and motivates people to go the extra mile.

success and eventual sale of the voice-mail business to MCI "gave them a pretty good little kick," he says. Shared values also have driven the family's successful venture-capital endeavors, including investments ranging from internet access provider Mindspring, to men's clothing and carpet tile concerns.

9. Executing strategy.

When strategy is a good fit with owners', managers' and employees' values, it is likely to be implemented with greater energy, enthusiasm and insight. Bringing values to life imparts passion and motivates people to go the extra mile. A strategy has to make business sense, of course. But when a choice must be made between a good strategy that meshes with shared values, and a better one that is less compelling from a values standpoint, we have found that the "good" strategy is actually a better choice. Assuming both strategies are sensible, the "good" one has a greater chance of success because it will tap participants' enthusiasm and draw out their most heartfelt effort.

10. Forging strategic alliances.

A strength of many family businesses is the value owners place on trust, integrity and loyalty. Family businesses typically aren't faceless, uncaring organizations driven by transient leadership and flavor-of-the-month strategy. The face of the family business is the family's face; its name is the family name. Family firms' long-term orientation makes them more likely to behave in ways that build commitment. The reputation of owners and their heirs

rests on the integrity of the business and its trustworthiness with key stakeholders.

These qualities make family businesses attractive venture partners, giving them a critical advantage in the global economy. In this era of strategic alliances, many companies are sharing technology, sales forces or marketing programs, or subcontracting parts of their operations. A stable, trustworthy family firm with a long-term orientation has a distinct competitive advantage in this environment. Also, family businesses that value trust tend to attract partners worthy of trust. Well-placed trust reduces the cost of doing business, eliminating the need for a lot of back-checking, lawyering and guarding one's flanks.

The Robert Mondavi Winery capitalizes on what it recognizes as these qualities unique to family businesses. In *Harvest of Joy: My Passion for Excellence,* Mondavi says he seeks family businesses as partners throughout the world. Moreover, he insists that partners be equals: "With a fifty-fifty split, neither side can impose a decision....and a fifty-fifty split builds cooperation and trust." His approach has gained him such partners as the Rothschilds of France, the Frescobaldis of Italy, and Chile's Chadwick family.

11. Recruiting and retaining employees.

Families that consistently honor the dignity and individuality of people lay the groundwork for an alluring workplace. Job seekers find respectful cultures attractive. New hires tend to stay longer. Employees are quicker to buy into their employer's objectives if they feel valued and respected as individuals. Workforce surveys show that such nonfinancial job attributes as "being treated with respect" are highly valued by workers. All this can afford a family business a coveted strategic advantage while holding down labor costs.

Motivated by service to what they consider to be meaningful goals, values are often part of the attraction for family members seeking to join and lead the business. Indeed, we find that when the older generation is deficient in communicating its value-based vision to the next generation, enthusiasm for sustaining the business is often lacking.

12. Lending meaning to work.

Family businesses with strong value systems have an edge in service or other labor-intensive businesses whose workers require a lot of hands-on operating discipline. Shared values, particularly when they focus on people-centered principles such as respect or

education and development, afford employees a sense of purpose that keeps them on track in even the most mundane jobs. A family retailing business with a people-centered ethic can instill in employees the inner discipline to provide caring customer service hour-to-hour, whether supervisors are present or not. Marriott and Meijer are examples of successful service businesses rooted in a strong belief in people by their owning families — a conviction that individuals will improve themselves, given the opportunity. People-centered values are the backbone of continuous-improvement and total quality management programs.

Why are values so powerful? Clearly, the kind of values we're talking about are more than empty slogans. They are like the taproots of giant plants that alter the landscape and the horizon for everyone in their circle of influence. Values shape feelings, thoughts and behavior in different ways at

Families that consistently honor the dignity and individuality of people lay the groundwork for an alluring workplace. Job seekers find respectful cultures attractive. New hires tend to stay longer. Employees are quicker to buy into their employer's objectives if they feel valued and respected as individuals.

different levels of human activity. On the most abstract level, all values spring from basic beliefs, such as: People are essentially good (or essentially bad); People exist to serve others (or to reap personal gain from them); Virtue is rewarded (or meaningless), And so on. Springing from these beliefs are values, the philosophies or tenets that bring beliefs one step closer to fruition. A belief that people are essentially good, for instance, is likely to lead the believer to place value on trust. Values, in turn, shape norms, the shared assumptions or guidelines about what constitutes right action or conduct. In business, valuing trust is likely to lead to a general practice, or norm, of disclosing information freely, as Burke did in the Tylenol crises. At the most concrete or visible level are the "artifacts" of values. Like the frescoed walls of an ancient civilization, artifacts are the symbols, possessions, products or stories that signify certain underlying beliefs and values in a family or business culture. The tales of employee heroics at Nordstrom are artifacts of the value the Nordstrom family places on empowering employees. A family business founder's framed "first dollar of profit" might be an artifact of the value placed on self-reliance or frugality. (Please see Exhibit A.)

Beyond the positive power of values in family business, values also hold the key to resolving some challenges innate to family business ownership. In the next chapter, we'll see how.

How Values Take Shape in Practice

BELIEFS: All values spring from basic beliefs.	Trusting others is a productive and rewarding way to live and do business. Information builds trust.	Self-reliance is the best security; (Or) Entrepreneurs make society better.	Human beings will take advantage of one another whenever possible.	What goes around comes around.	Families and businesses don't mix.
VALUES: Philosophies or attributes assigned fundamental significance.	Trustworthiness. Trust others when it is prudent to do so.	Independence and individuality.	Vigilance.	Long-term orientation.	Maximize current interests now.
NORM: A shared principle of right action or conduct.	All salaries and family gifts are disclosed.	Free choice. All lifestyles or career choices are accepted.	Verify all dealings and commitments.	Invest in the future. Weigh all decisions based on long-term effect.	Take advantage of favorable market conditions to sell the business.
ARTIFACT: Practices, prossessions, products or stories that serve as signs of underlying values.	Disclosure of financial information at annual meetings. A corporate annual report that discloses information even though the company is private.	Story about Grandpa's independence and how his self-reliance helped him survive the Great Depression.	Signed contracts on everything we do.	Story of how a handshake agreement produced a big return six years later.	Rule barring founder's children from jobs in the business. Stories about troubled business families.

II. *The Role of Values in Uniting Family and Business*

Family and business are so fundamentally different that they naturally pull apart over time.

Family and business have different short-term goals. Parents may want their children to lead the business, reap the biggest paychecks, be handed the best opportunities. Business needs to operate as a meritocracy. The family may need high dividends to thrive, while the business needs capital reinvested. The family may want all members included in the business, while the business needs to exclude unqualified employees. The business may need to fire a family member, a prospect that horrifies the family. The business may need to take on debt to grow, clashing with the family's desire for security and stability. The business may need a single CEO, while the family wants siblings or cousins to share power equally. (Please see Exhibit B.)

EXHIBIT B

Contrasting Realms of Business and Family

FAMILY GOALS	COMMON GROUND: *Shared Values*	BUSINESS GOALS
opportunity for all members		hire and promote on merit
pay to support well-being		pay for performance
equality		meritocracy
hire family		seek best-qualified applicant
family leadership succession		open to nonfamily executives
high dividends		reinvest capital
high profit		rapid growth
safety and security		risk-taking for growth

Rarely are financial incentives alone enough to unite a family split over such gut issues. There must be common ground that is stronger than the forces that pull family and business apart. Many families in search of this third dimension turn to shared values. Values are often the only glue strong enough. They work in four fundamental ways unique to families in business together:

1. Providing an incentive for sacrifice.

Owning a business together requires a lot of effort. Personal assets are at risk. Taxes seem unfair. Family members may resent the time and energy demanded of business leaders. The family name and reputation are under scrutiny in the workplace and in the community. Charities expect donations. The security of family members may be at risk. Almost every business owner asks, "Is it worth it?" At some point in almost every business-owning family's history, it seems more rational to sell the business and turn it into cash. Families may want to avoid the risk of disagreeing over some business issue and tearing themselves apart as a family. Individual members may decide it makes more sense financially to liquidate.

Families need a compelling rationale to get past these hurdles. A legacy of values is often the only goal worthy of all the effort and risk. As Chicago psychologist Susan Golden has found, an owner's satisfaction with involvement in the business is often a direct result of the fit between family values and the business. Similarly, **when the family sees the business exemplify its value system in the world at large, the practical relevance and power of sticking together becomes evident. This can fulfill two of the deepest human desires: To belong to something larger than ones' self, and to commit to a meaningful purpose. A legacy of values gives wealth — and life — meaning.**

2. Elevating the discussion.

Business families that find common ground in shared values often gain an inspiring and uplifting perspective. Identifying shared interests, finding the common good, is a powerful process. It elevates the discussion to a higher level that transcends day-to-day annoyances. It focuses participants on the positive. It gives members practice in shared decision making. And, assuming the process results in a statement of mission or values, as discussed in Part V, it gives families a sense of accomplishment in producing something concrete.

Common values become even more important as the business moves into second, third or fourth-generation family ownership. As the family disperses, shared values become a common lens through which members can envision a shared future. As was discussed in the book *The Trust*, the Ochs-Sulzberger family controlled the New York Times Co. through four separate trusts, each owned by a separate branch of the family. As fourth-generation cousins discussed the difficult question of how each would participate in decision making in the future, they realized that their intense, shared commitment to what the business stood for, including integrity, leadership and irreproachable excellence in its field, would be the glue that would keep them together. To fortify that glue, they formed task forces to work on philanthropy, setting up a family office, and family governance. Underpinning the work of each task force was the mission of manifesting the family's values in all its dealings with each other and with the outside world.

3. Generating a unique kind of synergy.

A family's values, exemplified in the business by leaders and employees steeped in the family ethos, can create a reciprocal energy that goes beyond the business benefits discussed in Part I. **Seeing shared values at work in the world at large can spark tremendous energy and enthusiasm in the family. Family members in turn tend to take a more patient, long-term view, lowering the business's cost of capital. A strong value system tends to improve business planning and decision making, to attract a stronger workforce and to strengthen the hand of business leaders in the marketplace. The family in turn takes pride in the strengths and image of the business. Family members are encouraged to undertake the work of further strengthening the family and assuring a shared legacy. As a result of that work, family members' behavior and cohesiveness improves, strengthening the cultural base of the business. Thus the best interests of the business serve the family, and the best interests of the family serve the business.** (Please see Exhibit C.)

EXHIBIT C ▐██████████████████████████████

Reciprocal Power of Values in Family and in Business

Family Realm	Business Realm

A Durable Value System that Benefits Both Realms

Sincerity and Genuineness in Manifesting Values

Improved Family Behavior

Important and Practical Values Exercised in the Business

Family Pride

Strength to Business

Founder(s)' Beliefs

4. Pruning the tree.

Values are an excellent basis for resolving ownership conflicts in the second and third generations and beyond. **Just as shared values among owners can strengthen a business, differences in values can cripple it.** Indeed, the family can become "a major threat to the company's success" if members fail to see a purpose beyond protecting the welfare of the family, says Warren Featherbone Co.'s "Gus"

> *Just as shared values among owners can strengthen a business, differences in values can cripple it.*

Whalen Jr. Without shared values, family members "feel disconnected from others in the company," Whalen writes in his book, *The Featherbone Principle: A Declaration of Interdependence.*

In such cases, the rule becomes "'We' and 'They,'" he says. "The family itself can become fractional and isolated, leading to a downward spiral in personal relationships within the family and within the company." He continues, "Any traditional family business has a greater chance of long-term survival when there is a vision greater than the business itself. A broader purpose. A sense of mission that is passed from one generation to the next. And members of the core family have to discover connections that exist between people inside and outside the company ...."

Thus the core question for relatives of all stripes, whether employed in the business or not, is, "Do we share common values and a desire to see them at work in the business?" A family member or in-law who answers "no" might do well to bail out, to avoid inevitable conflicts. On the other hand, even the most distant cousin who doesn't work in the business might find it meaningful to remain an owner if his or her answer is "yes." The family-business investment could be a vehicle not only for long-term financial gain, but for nostalgia and for teaching children certain values.

J. Smith Lanier says his family strengthened the business's ownership base by "pruning the tree" in this way. As the businesses entered the third and fourth generations of family ownership, shareholders' interests and values diverged, Mr. Lanier says. "Some people want income, some want to grow, some want salaries, some want dividends. When you get those conflicts, you need to face them and solve them as quickly as possible," he says. Mr. Lanier's immediate family bought out family members who didn't share core values and goals for the business. "You can't have some people who want to bleed the company and others that want to grow it," he says simply. In enlisting venture partners, Mr. Lanier says, the family doesn't accept investors unless they share the family's value system.

If values are so critical in family business, which values are the "right" ones? In the next chapter, we'll take a closer look at what makes "good" and "bad" values in the family business, and at some values that winning family businesses tend to share.

TABLE 2

VALUES AS THE GLUE IN FAMILY BUSINESS

1. Providing an incentive for sacrifice
2. Elevating the discussion
3. Generating a unique synergy
4. Pruning the tree

III. A Sampling of Winning Family Business Values

Many people assume, amid all the talk about values in political and business circles, that "values" are always something good.

We see "value" as a neutral term. It is neither automatically positive nor automatically negative. Audiences are startled by one example we cite, of families involved in organized crime. These families are rife with values: Only family can be trusted. Family interests must be protected at all costs — including committing murder if necessary. Loyalty to the family is valued above all, including interpersonal relationships and life itself. Obviously, these values foster a snarl of crime and injustice. A parallel example is the street gang that values loyalty so highly that it forces recruits to kill someone to be a member.

Even when they remain unspoken or unconscious, values based on prejudice or other counterproductive beliefs have great power to disrupt family business relationships and results. Some business owners value men over women in leadership roles. This may prevent them from picking the best-qualified candidate for succession or from allowing female shareholders an appropriate role. Promising women employees may be lost to the business, or female shareholders may revolt, splitting the family and undermining the business.

Some seemingly "good" values have bad effects.

One value that hurts many family businesses is, "We will maintain peace at all costs." This maxim may seem a plus while children are young. The ban on arguments keeps things quiet. It also can help sustain extended families through tough times. However, preventing conflict also prevents family members from resolving differences. Children grow up seeing any conflict as too risky. Offspring become so averse to conflict that they cannot resolve the natural tensions that arise from trying to run a business together.

> *Even when they remain unspoken or unconscious, values based on prejudice or other counterproductive beliefs have great power to disrupt family business relationships and results.*

23

As loyal and loving as these adult children may be, they are help-less to surmount the real disagreements that always arise in any healthy adult collaboration.

Striving for authenticity.

If values are so powerful, why not just make up some good ones? A business owner intent on long-term success as a family-owned en-terprise may wish, with the best intentions, to promote values that help the family and business along that path. But he or she can't sim-ply "make up" the "right" values. **True values arise from people's real experience, history and traditions. They can't be invented.**

All values have certain qualities, or they aren't values. They must be *authentic;* that is, they must spring from true, deeply held beliefs. *Built to Last* authors describe how leaders of the "best of the best" companies identified their core values: "They articulated what was inside them, what was in their gut, what was bone deep. It was as natural to them as breathing. It's not what they believed as much as *how deeply they believed it."* Values must be piercingly *simple,* able to be stated clearly in just one, two or three words. And they must be *resilient.* In helping businesses select the most powerful values, Collins and Porras recommend asking the following question: "Which of these values would we strive to live for a hundred years *regard-less* of changes in the external environment — *even* if the environ-ment ceased to reward us for having these values, or perhaps even penalized us?" Authentic values would survive this acid test.

Finding the root of synergy.

In family business, values also must be durable, resilient in changing times. The best values are robust, distinct and power-ful. They encompass as many dimensions of business and family behaviors as possible. In that, they create common ground.

Some family business owners believe, "Only family members can be trusted." As authentic as this value may be, it lacks the resiliency needed in business. While it may bind family members together, it can inhibit the family and the business by curtailing relationships with friends, community members, employees, customers, suppli-ers, lenders and investors. It cripples the business in any effort that requires expertise beyond the family's. And it damages the business's ability to forge new alliances in the marketplace. In the long term, it can severely limit the ability of both the family and the business to prosper.

Other family businesses are hurt by values that fail the test of changing times. The history of one venerable family-owned resort was rooted in a tradition of turning away non-WASP customers. Only rigorous efforts by successors to communicate their inclusive, unbiased policies finally eased the lingering effects of those values from the resort's image.

Families who succeed in nurturing more effective values often start by asking themselves, What are our family values? Then, they determine which of those values bring strength to the business. In turn, when certain values emerge in the business, the family may ask itself which ones instill pride and commitment in the family. This is the root of synergy. To the extent that the family's values bring strength to the business, the business will be more likely to grow and endure. To the extent that the business' values bring pride to the family and set a good example, the family will be stronger, more unified and more committed to the business.

In our experience, there are certain clusters of values that tend to underlie successful family businesses. Some or none of them may be values you share. However, they are examples of the kinds of values that create synergy. They encompass both the business and the family, they motivate people, they create productive results and they are durable enough to withstand change. Here is a sampling of twenty such values, summarized in Table 3.

TABLE 3 _____

SOME VALUES OFTEN FOUND IN SUCCESSFUL FAMILY BUSINESSES

1. Accountability
2. Adding value
3. Collective good
4. Valuing input and interaction (give and take)
5. Education and development
6. Ethical conduct
7. Focus on values and values education
8. Fun
9. Justice
10. Meritocracy
11. Openness
12. Practical realism
13. Risk-taking
14. Self-reliance
15. Servant leadership
16. Social purpose
17. Entrepreneurial spirit
18. Stewardship
19. Trust
20. Valuing stakeholders

1. Accountability.

Successful business families know members must be accountable for their actions to shareholders, employees and other stakeholders in the business. Otherwise, an "I'm a family member and I can do what I want" ethos may prevail, a permissive notion that opens the door to all kinds of exploitation of the business and the people who depend upon it. The damage this attitude can do is well-documented in the histories of great family business failures. In contrast, **the family that values accountability is more likely to produce business leaders willing to reach out for resources that enhance their chances of success.** These leaders are more likely to set up an independent board of directors, keep shareholders appropriately informed and set fair family compensation policies — all steps that we have found strongly increase a family business' survival chances.

2. Adding value.

To succeed, a business must consistently add value. Strong families often see their lives together in the same way, as they strive to build a legacy for future generations. **Adding value also gives individuals, both in the business and in the family, a sense of making a difference, of making a contribution. As one business-owning family leader put it, "I just tell my children to 'be useful' in some way."**

3. Collective good.

We have met many families who frequently retell the ancient parable of how a bundle of sticks is stronger than any single twig. The attitude this parable teaches, a willingness among family members to place the good of the family as a whole above their individual needs, can be a powerful tool for pursuing shared goals. **Healthy families still respect individual needs. But family members are clear that, when situations pit the needs of one individual against what's best for everybody, the collective welfare will prevail.** Such balancing acts are nearly universal in family business. Sibling rivalries, succession problems, family jealousies over compensation, arguments about dividends vs. reinvestment in the

The family that values accountability is more likely to produce business leaders willing to reach out for resources that enhance their chances of success.

business — all are rooted in the tension over valuing the whole over the sum of the parts.

4. Valuing Input and Interaction.

Family therapists say the characteristics that most often mark healthy, successful families are the capacity to make shared decisions and to communicate well. Successful business-owning families value both those skills. **Families who value input and interaction learn to ease difficult family decisions. They raise children equipped to air and resolve disputes. The mere process of sharing a decision empowers children, makes them believe their ideas are important and lays the groundwork for continuing success.**

Families who value input and interaction learn to ease difficult family decisions. They raise children equipped to air and resolve disputes. The mere process of sharing a decision empowers children, makes them believe their ideas are important and lays the groundwork for continuing success.

In the business, leaders who value input and interaction are more likely to seek the advice and counsel of independent directors, a step we have found greatly increases the chances of family business success. They are more comfortable consulting capable advisors. They build stronger executive teams and they work better with joint venture partners.

5. Education and development.

A wonderful example of the common denominator between family and business, education and development creates common ground by focusing on people. It gives rise to continuous skill-building and improvement in both the workforce and the family. Families who devote time to teaching communication and interpersonal skills are more likely to produce capable successors, both as leaders and owners. Cultivating a sense of responsibility around ownership and family membership builds cohesiveness in the family and strength in the business. Similarly, business leaders who invest in employee training and development are more likely to build a strong, winning culture and to attract and retain great people.

6. Ethical conduct.

Another excellent example of the synergy between business and family values, adherence to ethical conduct helps a business lure high-caliber executives, employees and advisors. A history of ethical conduct makes the business more attractive to outside investors or partners. A reputation for ethical conduct can actually attract new business opportunities in the form of partners looking for joint ventures or strategic alliances. On the family front, pride in ethical conduct and the good reputation it earns in the community can build cohesiveness and cement members' commitment to the business and the family alike.

Identifying, naming and planning to exercise shared values in the world at large can be the most bonding of family activities. It tends to produce a stronger ownership base. Cultivating core values among employees in the business has similar effects, building a more powerful business culture.

7. Focus on values.

The subject of this booklet, values and values education, is a focus common among successful family businesses. **Identifying, naming and planning to exercise shared values in the world at large can be the most bonding of family activities. It tends to produce a stronger ownership base. Cultivating core values among employees in the business has similar effects, building a more powerful business culture.**

8. Fun.

Values shared by successful families aren't all dead serious. **Many families place a high priority on having fun together. They plan time at family gatherings just for socializing and recreation. They may cultivate curiosity, creativity or nonconformity as explicit principles. These high-spirited values leaven the cultures of some of the strongest business families we know.**

9. Justice.

A focus on justice or fair process can ease decision making at all levels of the family business. Social science research shows people can accept a decision they oppose, if they believe the process of decision making was fair. If family members agree on fair processes for making such potentially divisive decisions as picking new leaders, divvying up capital, deciding who's in and who's out among shareholders and so on, they are much more likely to sustain the cohesiveness necessary for business success.

10. Meritocracy.

A well-established principle in business, meritocracy is likely to produce the best results in the marketplace. A culture of merit attracts and retains the most talented managers and employees. It fosters creativity and productivity. **In the family, valuing merit as a basis for business decisions also can become a way of thinking. If children are raised on this principle, they will have more realistic expectations about their future and a better understanding of meritocracy as a business strength. This makes the business attractive to the most capable family members.**

11. Openness.

Transparency is a value that builds strength over time in both the business and the family. Sharing information in the business helps educate family members to commit the financial resources necessary for business success. It aids strategic planning by giving trusted managers and directors the information they need to make wise decisions. It encourages ethical behavior. It aids estate planning by enabling co-owners of the business to coordinate ownership succession. In the family, this principle helps build trust over the generations. Its importance can best be seen in situations where families have failed to be open. For example, parents may make secret gifts to family members who aren't working in the business. Perhaps these family members have

> *Families who understand the need to take appropriate risks are far more likely to keep the business well-capitalized and to avoid arguments over draining cash as dividends or redeeming shares.*

chosen lower-paying occupations and the parents want to "make up for" that disparity, saying, "Don't tell your brother or sister I did this." Such gifts can cause tremendous conflict and resentment later, when parents are no longer present to preserve the veil of secrecy. Instead, the family can discuss the situation of family members who have financial needs and determine "fair" ways of responding to shared family goals.

*The degree to which **a** family business succeeds under multiple owners is often equal to the degree to which siblings or cousins embrace the principle of servant leadership.*

12. Practical realism.

As family and business leaders know, practical realism is basic to business and family survival. This principle means keeping your eye on the ball and being alert to the changing environment. It also means raising children to constantly assess and re-assess their circumstances in a clear-eyed fashion and react in mindful, skillful ways. Without this fundamental value, other initiatives are likely to fail.

13. Risk-taking.

Families who understand the need to take appropriate risks are far more likely to keep the business well-capitalized and to avoid arguments over draining cash as dividends or redeeming shares. Individuals may benefit in their personal lives, too, by availing themselves of new opportunities and experiences.

14. Self-reliance.

A value that drives many entrepreneurs and runs deep in many business families, it encourages hard work, initiative and creativity, and fosters self-discipline of a kind that can heighten a family business' chances of success.

15. Servant leadership.

Placing a higher value on helping others or helping the group achieve shared goals than on achieving your own individual desires is evidence of servant leadership. It contrasts with autocratic leadership, which places value on individual power, status and control over others. Servant leadership is especially important in a family business. Many businesses have not only multiple

30

owners, but multiple leaders as they pass to the next generation. **The degree to which a family business succeeds under multiple owners is often equal to the degree to which siblings or cousins embrace the principle of servant leadership.** This value vaccinates the family against ego-driven battles over titles, power or status. It enables family members to contribute based on their competencies, sometimes at varying levels over time as circumstances dictate. It fosters healthy teamwork among siblings or shareholders. And it serves as a compass for executives seeking to empower employees and create a human, balanced leadership style.

16. Social purpose.

A family business that sees itself as working to improve society can reap several practical benefits. The goodwill it earns can draw support from customers, employees and lawmakers. One business family in Central America has been able to survive and prosper through all kinds of governmental turbulence. Family members' bond with the public and their image as socially conscious citizens are so strong that no government wants to take them on. Also, family philanthropic ventures can support the business's strategy when focused on goals important to the business, such as education or school-to-work efforts.

As businesses pass into the third, fourth and fifth generation of family ownership, we have found the value that commits family shareholders most strongly to ownership is the belief that the family business is in some way making a meaningful difference to society.

Fulfilling a social purpose also enables the owning family to take pride in the business and forge a stronger sense of identity. This is a remarkably powerful effect over time. As businesses pass into the third, fourth and fifth generation of family ownership, we have found the value that commits family shareholders most strongly to ownership is the belief that the family business is in some way making a meaningful difference to society.

31

17. Entrepreneurial Spirit

Most family businesses were founded by entrepreneurs or enterprising individuals. These achievers exemplified creativity, self-reliance and making a difference. **Many successful families in business together cultivate this spirit and treat the business as a continuing inspiration.** They foster entrepreneurship in younger family members, sometimes through organized venture funds. The business benefits from this value, too, in increased quickness to capitalize on new markets and opportunities.

18. Stewardship.

An attitude toward ownership, we have found stewardship to be the most important value in families who are successful in passing businesses from one generation to the next. To be a good steward is to take personal responsibility for leaving resources better than they were when they came into your care. Stewardship springs from the ancient idea that the wise management and passing on of property and privilege is an honorable role that brings meaning and pride to the steward. An entrepreneur or owner who values stewardship believes it is his or her duty, responsibility and privilege to pass the business on to others, for them to build and serve in similar fashion, creating a process of multi-generational continual improvement and progress.

The opposite of stewardship is proprietorship. An owner who has a proprietary attitude believes, "This is my business, to do with whatever I wish. I invented the business. I suffered for the business. I built the business. If I want the business to serve my personal pleasure, I can have that. But if I don't, that's my decision too." Clearly, the values of stewardship and proprietorship are polar opposites. In proprietorship, the positive emphasis is on self. In stewardship, the positive emphasis is on benefitting

We have found stewardship to be the most important value in families who are successful in passing businesses from one generation to the next. To be a good steward is to take personal responsibility for leaving resources better than they were when they came into your care.

others in the future.

This central principle of stewardship explains more about the success of family business than any other single value. Business leaders who see themselves as proprietors will at some point, when they have all they need or want, have no reason to continue growing the business, taking risk, looking for opportunities. In contrast, **business leaders who value stewardship are truly committed to the perpetual growth of the business. They are motivated to continue to take risks, looking for opportunities and working extra hard, and they continually find meaning in doing so.**

Business owners who embrace stewardship are motivated to submit to the difficult process of succession. Stewardship encourages them to prepare a successor or successors. It helps them over the hurdle of giving up power in the business. It helps them take the difficult step of relinquishing control over the family. And it helps them teach younger family members to lead the way.

Business leaders who value stewardship are truly committed to the perpetual growth of the business. They are motivated to continue to take risks, looking for opportunities and working extra hard, and they continually find meaning in doing so.

An attitude of stewardship empowers business owners as parents, too. Families that believe in proprietorship risk creating a sense of entitlement in their children, because the perspective children see at work is a self-centered one. Families who believe in stewardship have an opportunity to pass on a more generous, future-directed perspective. This equips the children of successful, wealthy business families to cope better with inherited wealth and privilege.

19. Trust.

The ramifications of valuing trust are far-reaching. Essentially, trust is a kind of valve that opens up family firms to the broadest possibilities for building a strong family and a strong business. Families in business together who can trust outsiders are able to seek competent nonfamily executives when none is available in the family. They can reach out to skilled advisors. They are attractive to venture partners, and they are more likely to establish excellent, independent boards of directors.

Families who can trust also are better equipped to think long-term — one of the family business's most important competitive advantages. Members are confident that everyone's interests will be taken into account over time. They are unlikely to be distracted by worries about what they or a relative are getting out of the business today. Trust enables family members to benefit from the counsel of advisors and directors. Children who grow up among adults who can trust also are more likely to avoid a pitfall for the offspring of wealthy families: A disproportionate, sometimes paralyzing fear that others will take advantage of them. They are better able to accept the privileges, responsibilities and risks of wealth without guilt, fear or suspicion, particularly when "trust" and "practical realism" are both highly valued.

20. Valuing stakeholders.

Tending the interests of all of a business's stakeholders — employees, customers, shareholders, suppliers and the community — can yield a family business advantage. Valuing stakeholders tends to protect the business from bureaucracy because it ensures an external, rather than an internal, focus. And it can bolster performance. In research presented in their book, *Corporate Culture and Performance,* John Kotter and James Heskett found the most adaptive, successful cultures consistently valued not just stockholders, but multiple stakeholders. That focus helped businesses see and respond more quickly to changes in the competitive climate, figure out new strategies and continually satisfy customers, owners and employees. The result: Financial performance outstripped that of other companies many times over.

Family first? Or business first?

This brings us to a larger question faced by many families in business together: Are we a "family first" enterprise or a "business first" enterprise? Ideally, as we have discussed, both are true. The welfare of the business feeds the welfare of the family, and *vice versa.* But serving both family and business simultaneously isn't an easy balance to achieve. Often, families reach a stage where they must reconcile conflicts.

In our work with hundreds of family businesses, we've seen the most successful among them agree on a delicate balancing act: Family is first, but the family must *act as if* the business comes first. Why? Because running a successful business serves the goals and needs of the family. *Acting* as if the business comes first requires the family to stick to a set of values that are healthy for family members as well. Running a business requires discipline, for example, and that can be good for the family. Family business shareholders must sometimes put the good of the group ahead of individual wants and needs —another positive value. They must also be willing to accept temporary discomfort in pursuit of longer-term goals, a discipline that can enhance the long-term quality of personal lives. Thus the business becomes the shared tool that hones the collective well-being of the family.

Finding the right balance.

Pursuing one value to extremes can damage both a business and its owners. Former turnaround hero "Chainsaw Al" Dunlap adhered famously to the value of efficiency by laying off thousands of employees at companies he ran. He met his Waterloo at Sunbeam, however, when his cost-cutting hatchet fell too hard. After he was fired by Sunbeam's board amid questions about earnings quality, his successors suggested Dunlap had driven Sunbeam's staff too hard and slashed management ranks too deeply in pursuit of unrealistic targets. Critics said he also had lost focus on Sunbeam's customers — a core value in a company built on trademark consumer brands. The example shows the importance of embracing a balanced set of synergistic values.

Ideally, values in a business operate as a system, inter-reliant and mutually supportive. In his excellent book, *Business As A Calling,* Michael

In our work with hundreds of family businesses, we've seen the most successful among them agree on a delicate balancing act: Family is first, but the family must act as if the business comes first. Why? Because running a successful business serves the goals and needs of the family. Acting as if the business comes first requires the family to stick to a set of values that are healthy for family members as well.

Novak cites the "three cardinal virtues" of business as creativity, building community and practical realism. Each of these good habits requires the support of other good habits. Creativity requires courage, hard work and persistence. Building community requires honesty and generosity. Practical realism demands the capacity for self-understanding and self-correction. Thus, values are the matrix for an adaptive, dynamic corporate culture.

Another dilemma faced by some family businesses is that the stronger and more compelling the values they embrace, the higher the likelihood that some family members will disagree with them. If a family's values are extremely distinct, pronounced or potentially controversial, they are likely to cause disagreement or force some family members to exit the business. If this is the case, it becomes important to have policies allowing for the graceful exit of family members, such as buyout plans. A family whose values rest heavily and specifically on certain religious principles, for instance, may find over the generations that allowing some members to exit quietly is essential to family peace.

Family leaders must strike a careful balance here. Successful families value the potential richness of individual differences, collaboration and compromise. On the other hand, it's important to focus on values that are powerful and meaningful enough to make a difference. The art here is in having values that have enough power to unite the family and the business, but not so much that they extend into the realm of dogma.

Ideally, a family can focus on values that encompass both the business and the family. These are values that make a difference, but are also durable, appropriate and distinct. Like the strongest family businesses, such values tend to endure through changing environments.

How do business-owning families articulate and transmit these important values? The processes in family and business are parallel in many ways. In the next two chapters, we'll discuss some methods and techniques many family business leaders have used successfully.

IV. Nurturing and Passing on Values in the Family

Where do values come from, and how do they take root and endure in families? **Families begin transmitting values very, very early, often before consciously realizing they are doing so. Parents teach values mainly by living them. This process begins almost at birth.** It may be intentional or unintentional. After the husband-and-wife owners of one family business greeted the birth of their youngest child, they brought their older son, then five years old, to the hospital to see the new baby. The little boy expected to see his mother with the infant in her arms. Instead, when he entered her room, he saw his baby brother lying in a bassinet beside her bed. His first image of his mother after this historic event was of her lying in a hospital bed cradling not an infant, but a duplicate invoice book. She was making sure all the family business accounts were up-to-date.

> *Families begin transmitting values very, very early, often before consciously realizing they are doing so. Parents teach values mainly by living them. This process begins almost at birth.*

The value at work: It doesn't matter what else is going on in your life. You do your work. Obviously, neither parent in this case had consciously decided to teach their son that lesson. But it came through loud and clear.

Children are not only keen observers, but avid questioners on matters relating to values. Their innate desire to make sense of life often emerges in "why" questions. Why do you go to work? Why do we go to church? Why do I have to do (fill in the blank)? As annoying as children's questions may be, the answers often unearth core values. The children are looking for principles to help them shape their own behavior, and ultimately, their choices, in the future.

Among adults in the family business, core questions about values often take similar form. Why do we work so hard in the business? Why should we make financial sacrifices so the business can grow? Why should we strive so hard to hold the family together? None of these questions can be answered by whipping out a profit and loss statement or a one-minute management guide. The answers

can be found only in the realm of values. Families who take time to teach children the "why" of achieving the goals they desire, rather than simply the "what" and "how," are far more likely to produce adults capable of answering these questions and sustaining family business ownership. This teaching should begin at as young an age as possible. Various families handle this process in various ways.

The early years. In his book on how wealthy families impart values and attitudes about wealth to their children, *The Charitable Impulse,* James A. Joseph cites research showing that simply giving lip service to altruistic values is not enough to teach children compassion and generosity. Instead, parents who succeeded on this front followed a specific pattern of child-rearing. They exerted firm control over their children's moral development. They actively guided them to do good, to share and to be helpful. These parents also reinforced the values they wished to teach by exposing children to religion or institutions that espoused them. Both parents and these institutions told stories to the children that exemplified the values. Joseph wrote, "Our children must learn from us at an early age that if the strong exploit the weak, or the rich ignore the needy, the future of our society is gravely impaired."

Among adults in the family business, core questions about values often take similar form. Why do we work so hard in the business? Why should we make financial sacrifices so the business can grow? Why should we strive so hard to hold the family together? None of these questions can be answered by whipping out a profit and loss statement or a one-minute management guide. The answers can be found only in the realm of values.

The Rauenhorst family, owners of Opus Corp., a Minnesota-based developer that has been recognized by its industry for quality, began early to instill productive values in second-generation family owners. The family taught youngsters by example to keep money in perspective. Elders avoided conspicuous consumption, reinvested profit in the business and quietly

38

donated substantial amounts to charity. The family also encouraged professional management and smooth succession by assigning high value early to education, including education about the family business. As the children grew up, the Rauenhorsts encouraged teamwork. Adults also exemplified family unity by sharing interests outside the business.

A family's values are evident in adult members' character. Yoshimi Shibata, the second-generation president of a family nursery business, saw in his father, the founder, a strong example of robust, powerful values. Shibata learned spiritual discipline from his father through kendo, the martial art of sword fighting. Studying kendo had "a very profound effect on my life," teaching him endurance, good observation and a strong offense, Shibata says. Later, his father taught them the value of self-reliance in a creative way: He offered each child $1 if they could make a little boat sail across the garden pond, or build a model airplane that would stay in the air for five minutes.

Hard work was a value Shibata's father taught by example. He remembers watching his father work from before dawn until after dark, organizing tasks based on the amount of daylight needed. Bunching flowers, for instance, was done at night, to avoid wasting valuable daylight.

In one particularly difficult life lesson, his father also passed on the principle of resiliency. When the family was forced into an internment camp during World War II, and the four Shibata sons were drafted into the U.S. military, his father reminded a distraught Yoshimi, "We will build again. This is not the end, just a bad storm." As he watched his father move the business to the best location for growing flowers, he learned that mobility could be a blessing. Bringing joy to others was another value, one that underlay all of his father's work. Regardless of how chaotic the world became, Shibata saw how his father's work, and his own, could make others a little happier.

Even the simplest youth activities can teach children lessons that reverberate in adult life. Coaching kids' teams, leading scouting troops or taking part in other volunteer endeavors can be an excellent way to teach valuing the collective interests of the group over individual self-interest, a value common to many successful business families. One father taught his son to place the best interests of the group above his own by coaching his Little League team. When the son badgered his father to take him off the bench or let him play a favorite position, the coach replied: "We're going to do what's best for the team." The son eventually became president of the family business. When circumstances called for him to step down to make room for an executive with different strengths, his father, then chairman, aided the decision by reminding him, "Son, remember the Little League days." The transition was difficult, but that fundamental value made it possible to keep the family working as a family.

EXHIBIT D ▮▮▮▮▮▮▮▮▮▮▮▮▮▮▮▮▮▮▮▮▮▮▮▮▮▮▮

Values Education, as Seen at Cargill

Harry Martin recently retired as president of the family office for the Cargill/MacMillan family, controlling owners of Cargill Inc., named by *Forbes* magazine the world's largest privately owned family business. In an address to a private investors' conference, Martin stressed the importance of imparting to children the inner discipline needed to regard their wealth as a responsibility rather than a privilege. "This is a daunting task for wealthy families, since wealth often operates as an enemy to a child's positive development," Martin said. Wealth can deprive a child of opportunities to develop competency and character, offering "indulgent escapes from the need to experience hard work," success and failure, Martin said. "Problems are created when families give enormous emphasis to the creation of wealth, but don't give enough attention to the creation of a sound family able to manage it," Martin said. **"Money achieves value only through the use made of it. That wholly depends on the human qualities of those who create, perpetuate and utilize it."**

Martin named "the discipline of helping one's children create self-worth" as essential to successful transmission of both wealth, and a family business, across the generations. Children who are allowed to develop discipline in their lives and their work are better equipped to truly value any wealth or opportunities they may inherit, rather than using them as a route to self-indulgence or escape. "Wealth will be a scant solace later to the adult who as a child was never allowed to develop discipline in his life or work," Martin said. The best human qualities are developed by holding children to demanding standards — requiring them to "work hard, get good grades, be disciplined, get along in school, and if they don't — suffer the consequences," Martin said. "You'll know you've succeeded when your children regard their wealth as a responsibility, rather than as a privilege. You'll know you've succeeded when they have the character and competence to manage this responsibility."

In the business as well, inner discipline, instilled in successor generations in their youth, is "the bedrock for a smooth transition thirty to fifty years later," Martin said. The result of a successful generational transition is worth all the effort.

Sparking a multigenerational focus.

In extended families with adult children, the process of values education may move beyond parents. One or more adults typically take a leadership role. A member of the senior generation, such as a grandfather, founder or retired CEO, may initiate work on values. Sometimes, a wife, mother or grandmother acts as a catalyst. A sibling or cousin may develop an interest in values. Sometimes, a family member charged with writing a family history, or creating and keeping a family archive, becomes interested in the principles that guided family members through the generation. In other cases, an active board of directors or a trusted professional advisor may ask questions about the direction of the business that prompt the family to examine deeply felt values and goals.

Sometimes, one individual in a family serves as such a strong embodiment of a particular value that he or she sparks a family focus on the topic. For example, Kacie LaChapelle and Louis Barnes found in a study published in *Family Business Review* (March, 1998) that one person in the family can establish trust as a transgenerational norm. This "trust catalyst," the authors said, accomplishes this in several ways. She may model trusting behavior, extend the integrity of the family to dealings with non-family and safeguard the rights of both. She also personifies character, competency, predictability and caring, the building blocks of trust in personal relationships.

Many families find that cherished old stories, told and retold at family gatherings, start family members talking about values. These stories typically have strong underlying morals. One son in a family-owned retailing business recalls his father saying, "The whole secret to retailing is putting the key in the lock at 6 a.m." Behind this folksy maxim is the strong value this business owner placed upon hard work and anticipating the competition.

Many families find that cherished old stories, told and retold at family gatherings, start family members talking about values.

41

Another axiom from the same business owner, recalled by his son: "Only let family members handle cash. That way, if somebody is stealing from you, at least it's going for a good cause." That homey witticism springs from a constellation of values, from "The business exists to serve the family," to "Be wary of whom you trust."

In larger families, a more structured approach is sometimes needed to unearth shared values. Some families begin by meeting with a facilitator. One approach is to break the family into small groups and ask each to tell the stories about the family and the business that they remember most vividly. The facilitator may ask, "When you think of the founder (or another business or family hero), what stories come to mind? What are the three stories you remember most?" Another technique is to ask family members to take turns finishing the sentence, "My daddy (or granddaddy) used to say ..." or "Momma used to say ...." Back in a large group, the facilitator may identify key words or phrases in the stories that are told, such as "giving back," "privacy" or "helping others." These can be written down on Post-It notes and clustered together, based on their meaning, on display boards. As patterns of emphasis emerge, so do the values that underlie the stories. It's usually best to trim the list of important values to the six to twelve tenets that are most robust and hold the most potential for integrating the mission and goals of the family and the business.

Whose values will prevail?

A potential obstacle to this work is mistrust. A powerful matriarch or patriarch who habitually preaches certain values to the kids may have erased trust in any attempt at consensus. Second or third generation family members may fear that any gathering to focus on "the family's values" will be used by a family leader as a platform to pontificate on his or her own values. "Oh no, is this going to be another sermon on the work ethic?" they may say. "Is this going to be another chance for our parent to tell us that we're lazy, or that we have to lead by example?" This can be a damaging setback.

The founder or senior family member may have to take a back seat in the discussions to avoid this. Younger members must feel they have a genuine opportunity to shape decision making. Allowing younger family members to identify important values has an advantage for senior members, too. It gives them a chance to see how adult children view and interpret the examples they have set. A trained facilitator is important to make sure these sessions go well and all voices are heard. Also, the family needs to agree up front on a consensus-building process.

Passing on shared values.

Once consensus is reached on shared values, families can use a variety of techniques for bringing them to life and passing them on:

■ *Writing family creeds.* Some families work together to create values statements, mission statements, mottos or codes of conduct. These written documents are good reminders for everyone, and the process of writing them reinforces the values they express. Some families write their creeds beautifully in calligraphy or have them professionally printed, then frame them and hang them at strategic places. Examples of three families' statements of values are contained in the Appendix.

■ *Holding family meetings.* This can be an excellent medium for teaching values and putting them into action. Some families begin family meetings around the dinner table when children are young, with a goal of teaching values. Other families with older children spend time discussing such questions as, "What responsibility do I have to give back some of my wealth to the community? What philanthropic goals do we believe in?" (For information on family meetings, please see No. 2 in The Family Business Leadership Series, *Family Meetings: How to Build a Stronger Family and a Stronger Business.*) The act of gathering as a family in itself encourages members to recognize the principles and beliefs they share.

■ *Telling stories.* Again, family stories and parables are an excellent way to pass on established values in families of all kinds and sizes. Family leaders can make a point of including family stories in informal conversations or talks at family gatherings of all kinds.

■ *Arranging fireside chats.* Members of the senior generation in some families hold fireside chats with the youngest family members, talking about values and stories that illustrate them. Although parents can do this with their own children, these sessions are particularly powerful when grandparents sit down with grandchildren. "What does integrity mean to you?" the elder may ask the kids. "Let me tell you some stories." Or a senior family member may hold a Socratic discussion, drawing out and shaping the children's views through careful questioning. Videotapes of these sessions can be a powerful teaching tool for future generations.

■ *Conducting educational seminars.* Other families hold educational seminars on values. Family members may meet to discuss trust or the entrepreneurial spirit, for instance. They may bring in a speaker or discussion leader to enrich and guide the talks. The content of these gatherings can be tailored to suit any age group, including children. Another technique is to have one family member talk about a particular value and how it shaped his or her life.

■ *Organizing an active board.* Experienced independent family business directors, such as other business owners, can help the family work on values. Directors may serve as a resource or sounding board for family ideas and questions on values. They can encourage family leaders to undertake values education. And as respected, objective advisors to family shareholders, they can provide examples of values in action. (For more information on active boards, please see No. 8 in The Family Business Leadership Series, *Family Business Governance: Maximizing Family and Business Potential.*)

■ *Setting up a "family university."* Structuring a learning center for family members can be an effective route to values education and development. The family university may or may not have a physical location. Either way, it serves as a vehicle for organizing seminars, talks or ongoing programs for family education and development. Topics may include communication, listening, decision making or conflict resolution skills, as well as work on values. Whatever the focus, the mere existence of a family university can symbolize the value a family places on education and development of people. Families that sponsor shared learning often have the same kinds of programs operating in their businesses, in the form of training and development centers or company universities.

■ *Introducing children to the business.* Senior members of some families take children on business trips and make a point of showing them examples of the family's values at work in the business. Others have children attend store openings and hear family members make speeches about the guiding principles the family instills in the business.

■ *Writing an ethical will.* Some leaders of family businesses are embracing an ancient custom: "Ethical wills." These documents express the author's view of life's meaning and articulate a hoped-for legacy of values and beliefs. (Please see Exhibit E.)

*Guidelines for Writing an Ethical Will**

An ethical will is a letter or codicil to a legal will that bequeaths a spiritual or philosophical legacy. It may be read before or after the author's death or passed from generation to generation. While no prescribed format is necessary, here are some possible subjects:

— The important lessons learned during your life.

— People and causes for which you feel a sense of responsibility.

— Mistakes in your life you hope your children will avoid.

— Your definition of true success.

— Your hopes for loved ones' future regarding family unity, ethical conduct, charity, or business relationships.

— Favorite sayings or stories.

— Expressions of gratitude, hope or faith.

*From *So That Your Values Live On — Ethical Wills and How to Prepare Them,* edited by Rabbi Jack Riemer and Nathaniel Stampfer. Available from Jewish Lights Publishing, P.O. Box 237, Sunset Farm Offices, Route 4, Woodstock, VT 05091. Phone: 802-457-4000.

Laying a foundation for ownership.

Families in business together sometimes ask, "Do you teach the same values to children who will be working in the business as to those who will play only an ownership role in the future?" This raises some fundamental issues in family business ownership.

Families are often advised to take a narrow view, preparing certain children for leadership in the business and restricting ownership to them. The rationale is that people employed in the business are likely to have different values than those not employed in the business. Employees are more likely as owners to share the same goals, thereby strengthening the shareholder base and reducing the business's cost of capital.

That reasoning is true as far as it goes. **If, however, a family makes a conscious effort to instill in all children robust, shared values of the kind we are discussing in this book, such as stewardship, servant leadership, ethical conduct or adding value, those who grow up in an owner-only role can serve a powerful purpose.** Free of the pressures and expediencies of running day-to-day operations, these owners can provide a calm, clear reading on whether the business is adhering to shared values. By articulating and personifying those values themselves, they can serve as an example of the business's unique strengths. Both these roles send a powerful message to other stakeholders employees, customers, suppliers and the community — that can yield major competitive and cultural advantages.

If family makes a conscious effort to instill in all children robust, shared values of the kind we are discussing in this book, such as stewardship, servant leadership, ethical conduct or adding value, those who grow up in an owner-only role can serve a powerful purpose.

V. Building Values in the Business Culture

Sam Walton's father was an avid trader who bargained hard for low prices in the Depression-era dust bowl of Oklahoma and Missouri. The late Mr. Walton took that core value and transformed it into Wal-Mart, a retailing empire built around serving the customer with low prices. The same value drove his relentless insistence on squeezing costs out of the merchandising system, and his continual listening to customers that kept Wal-Mart attuned to its markets.

It didn't hurt, of course, that Mr. Walton was highly charismatic. He once donned a grass skirt and danced the hula on Wall Street when Wal-Mart's profit surpassed forecasts. And his unannounced visits to meet nearly all of the 345,000 employees in Wal-Mart's far-flung stores were legendary. But the values he embodied, painted on the sides of Wal-Mart's trucks ("We sell for less, always!") and instilled in Wal-Mart's culture, were what endured after his death and drove the chain's success.

Values in a family business often come from the founder or another strong, charismatic figure — the hero or heroes of the business. Other times, it falls to successor generations to identify the values that drive the business and bond the family to them. These leaders are prompted by a variety of events or circumstances, and they use a variety of methods. This chapter covers the who, when and how of values on the business side of the family business equation. It will discuss which individuals tend to take the lead in identifying and fostering values in the business, and at what stages of business development that tends to happen. And it will give tips on techniques business leaders use to nurture and perpetuate values.

The leadership role.

Often, work on values and values education starts with a family business founder. Early in the life of a business, the founder may have little time to do more than exemplify values. But as the business grows, he or she earns the opportunity to think more broadly. Many founders realize they're engaged in something bigger and more meaningful than carving out a living. New purposes emerge around achieving certain social goals or showing how human interrelationships work.

Explaining the remarkable success of *Built to Last,* the business bestseller on values and culture, co-author James Collins told *Inc.*

magazine in 1997 that people are "hungry to build something of enduring character on a fundamental set of virtues they can be proud of. They want to leave a legacy."

Assuring a legacy of values becomes an ideal role for the founder as the next generation assumes leadership of the business. This focus allows the founders' presence to endure in the most powerful sense. No longer the business head, or even its heart, he or she becomes its soul, the embodiment of its culture and values, the repository of history and memory. The day after Home Depot founder Bernard Marcus stepped down as CEO, he spoke with Roberto Goizueta, the late CEO of Coca-Cola. Marcus told Goizueta that they were each the soul of their companies, and souls live on forever. (*Atlanta Journal & Constitution,* May 31, 1997.)

Ultimately, founders who allow themselves to become the soul of the business do not even need to stick around. They become part of every living participant in the business, offering inner guidance and helping each correct course when he or she goes astray.

As Sam Walton's example shows, a founder's values may already permeate the culture of the business. He or she may have a particular, highly personal way of interacting with the marketplace and wresting from it some resounding success. A founder who is an engineer might instill reverence for innovation, creativity or product usefulness. A founder who is an extraordinary salesman might foster a value of quick response to customers' needs. **A leader who wants to be remembered for certain practices will freeze the company culturally, paralyzing it in the face of change. In contrast, a leader can liberate the organization and his or her successors by imparting a value system that endures through the generations.**

The chief emotional officer.

Work on values also can begin with another family member. Often, it's the founder's wife who sees the wisdom of identifying and writing down shared values. The family may be in a meeting, discussing how the business is faring, and she may say, "It's important that the business succeeds. But it's even more fundamental that we stick together." She may begin a dialog aimed at finding core values that unite the family and the business and become a foundation for moving ahead.

The successor.

Entrepreneurial founders are sometimes so busy building the business that any values they exemplify remain unspoken, unwritten and perhaps even unconscious. The values may be obvious to children and grandchildren; a strong belief in, say, quality, hard work, embracing change or valuing people may underlie nearly every decision the founder makes. But the entrepreneur and the family may never speak or even think of them as values.

Whether values are articulated or not, a successor who ignores a successful founder's value system is making a mistake. It can be a powerful tool for doing a good job, building on successes and fortifying the culture of the business. Identifying, articulating, writing down and integrating values into the culture of the business can strengthen and unite management. Also, when a team of siblings inherits the business, shared values can provide a rationale for succession and cooperation. They become the basis for going forward together.

The third generation and beyond.

Work on values can become crucial in the third generation of family ownership and beyond. Family businesses typically take one of two paths by this point. Without a strong value system as a foundation, many migrate toward the norms governing public companies. Maximizing shareholder value becomes the overriding goal, and stock price and liquidity are owners' focus. In time, these Wall Street-style values typically undermine the strengths particular to family business, such as the patience to pursue long-term goals or the commitment to stable, trustworthy bonds with stakeholders. Eventually, such family businesses begin to look, act and operate much like public companies. Values planning and education are essential if the maturing family business is to avoid this path. When we begin working with families in business together to plan for continuity, values are the starting point for decision making. Before any family gets too far along in planning, they must decide what they want to accomplish and why.

Triggering the discussion.

Certain events in the history of a family business tend to start people talking about values. Sometimes, anniversaries of the business are the catalyst. Another spark may be a decision to record family business stories while the founder is still alive to tell them. Often, questions about leadership and ownership succession are a starting point. Families may need to step back and examine their desire and commitment to own the business. A fundamental difference in family members' world view may crop up over strategy, succession, employment policy, allocation of capital or other matters.

Should family members get special treatment in hiring and promotion? Should the business pay bigger dividends to family or plow more capital into growth? Taking on debt for a promising acquisition, picking a new CEO, integrating new in-laws into the family —all can raise the question, "Are we on the same page here?" If differences on values run deep, striving for agreement on details may be fruitless. Without a strong rationale for continuing ownership across the generations, the chances of success are dim.

Assuring a legacy of values becomes an ideal role for the founder as the next generation assumes leadership of the business. This focus allows the founder's presence to endure in the most powerful sense. No longer the business head, or even its heart, he or she becomes its soul, the embodiment of its culture and values, the repository of history and memory.

In one case, a third-generation family business successor prepared to assume leadership of the business. But he sensed resentment and a feeling of disenfranchisement among family members who were not employed in the business. He arranged for his generation to take time to tell and listen to each other's most deeply felt beliefs. In that effort, he hopes to uncover shared family values that could be the foundation for a new, higher level of management accountability to owners not employed in the business.

In other cases, the succession decision itself may trigger conflict. For example, a young woman who is the most qualified based on her resume and track record, to lead the family business — say, a highly motivated MBA with a strong management track record outside the family business — may start a discussion of why the family is considering only men as potential successors, focusing on the question, "Do we value traditional gender roles over merit?" The outcome may be a shift to meritocracy, or a lasting rift. Either way, some discussion of values is essential.

In other cases, discussions about values arise when family members who are not active in the business seek a meaningful role. Fourth-generation owners of one large family business, representing four branches of the owning family, sought a voice in governance. Meeting with a consultant, they divided all the issues they faced into two

50

categories, one concerning the business, and a second concerning how to keep the family together. They called these categories "Family Business" and "Family Glue." Three task forces were named in each area. Each task force researched its topic and wrote a report.

One principle emerged from all six task forces as the uniting force, or "glue": "We are one family." The cousins realized it was their passionate, shared commitment to the values the family business stood for — integrity, leadership in its field and extraordinarily high-quality products — that would keep them together. Those shared values provided the foundation for a renewed commitment to the business and for new discussions with third-generation leaders of the business on what role the fourth generation would take.

Planning for values in the business.

Ideally, the process of bringing values to life in a family business starts with the owning family. As part of writing a family mission statement, the family may identify values that are relevant and helpful to the business.

For help clarifying values applicable to the business, some families ask nonfamily managers for their perspective. What values do these managers see at work in the business? What would the manager tell a family member who is being hired for the first time about what it takes to succeed in the business? What tips would the manager provide? The answers are often a revelation to the family. Outside advisors — trusted lawyers, accountants or consultants to the family business — also might be asked to compare and contrast the family business with others. How are its core principles like or different from others'? How is our family business seen by the man or woman on the street? What does the outside world say about us? What is our reputation? Answers can yield powerful insights. Families may learn they are seen as tough negotiators, generous but frugal, and so on.

Once the family is clear on its mission, philosophy and values, the next step is a statement of the nature of the family's commitment to the business. This statement becomes the basis for all family policies and plans, ranging from which family members are entitled to ownership to how the family will foster unity in the future. Finally, the family may state, in an owners' pledge, what the family is willing to offer to the business and what family members expect in return. The owners' pledge, for instance, might say, "We expect the business to be faithful to our value system. In return, we will put our shared values into practice in everyday life." The diagram in Exhibit F shows how this process works.

Family Continuity Planning Process

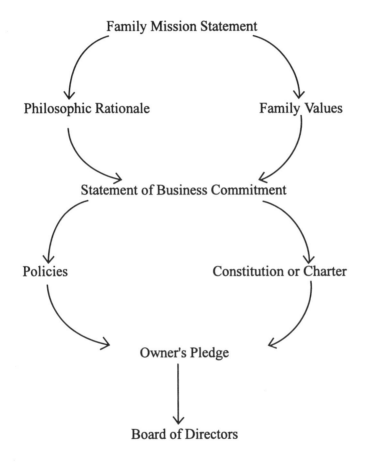

©John L. Ward 1996

This planning process takes shape in various ways. One family in its third generation of business ownership began working on values as members prepared to hand the business over for the first time to a nonfamily CEO. The family wanted to maintain ownership and close contact with the business and needed an explicit rationale for doing so. In a beautifully printed "family compact," the family stated its values: Respect for people, integrity, personal responsibility and trust. Drawing on scripture and quotes from religious settings, the family also stated its intent to practice stewardship, including preserving business values that had enabled the company to survive and prosper. It outlined the future role of family members not working in the business, including serving on the board and acting as "ambassadors" for the business. It laid out employment policy for family members entering the business. Each family member signed this compact.

One year later, the family revised and refined the compact to reflect the evolution of members' thinking. The new edition made the family's vision, values and mission even more specific, stating clearly and specifically how the family's values might be exercised in the operation of the business. For example, the compact stated that respect for people should be reflected by policies that empower employees and provide attractive compensation and benefits. The value placed on trust should be reflected in long-term relationships and joint initiatives with customers. The value placed on integrity should be reflected in business policies and practices that "honor the family name," the compact said. At this stage, the family also added a fifth value, renewal, to reflect the value placed on continuous improvement.

Communicating values in the business.

Family businesses use a variety of methods to communicate values in the business.

The corporate creed. The most basic step is to write a formal creed, or a statement of mission or values. This might be displayed prominently in the business, printed in employee communiques or engraved on wallet cards. At Warren Featherbone Co., a family business founded in 1883, a corporate creed states seven fundamental values and a sevenfold pledge to stakeholders arising from those values. (Please see Exhibit G.)

Warren Featherbone Company Corporate Creed

Leaders of this fourth-generation family business cite seven values that have guided it through 115 years of adaptation and success:

—Creative thinking

—Finding a need and filling it

—Focusing on value for customers

—Focusing on people at all levels of the process

—Maintaining enthusiasm —Working hard

—Maximizing the company's ability to adapt

Based on these seven values, Warren Featherbone has developed the following "Corporate Creed" governing dealings with all its constituencies, or stakeholders:

Warren Featherbone sees its Corporate Creed as its responsibilities to seven segments of our society. Fundamental to our relationship to these groups is the basic premise that fair and honest dealings should be a cornerstone on which all relationships are built.

*To consumers, we pledge consistent high quality and workmanship sold at a fair price. We will be aware of the needs of customers for attractive, well-fitting, comfortable and safe garments.

*To retail customers, we pledge consistently high quality products sold at a fair price, which can be re-sold at a fair profit for our retailers. We further pledge efficient sales support, order handling and delivery.

*To employees, Warren Featherbone Company believes that the "family image" of our business has helped to produce the success which we have enjoyed for over 100 years. People make the company, and not vice-versa. In view of this, Warren Featherbone intends to manage the business in a caring manner, providing the best work conditions possible, fair compensation, job security and the ability to advance according to one's initiative and talents.

*To suppliers, Warren Featherbone desires to promote a professional partnership with the suppliers who provide for our manufacturing needs. Our responsibilities include the expectation to receive the highest quality products and our willingness to pay a fair price for same. Our intent is to continue the same longlasting relationships with our suppliers that we enjoy with our retail customers.

*To the community, in which Warren Featherbone operates, our intent is to be a good corporate citizen, paying our fair share of local taxes and providing for significant and stable employment. We further wish to contribute the leadership of the members of our Company to civic affairs, to provide funds for worthy organizations and in every way, to be a good neighbor.

*To the environment, Warren Featherbone pledges not only its desire to be a pollution-free producer, but also to help better the surroundings in which its facilities are located. We feel the responsibility to build attractive buildings compatible with the local environment and preserve beauty in every way that we can.

*To Local, State and Federal Government, Warren Featherbone pledges itself to be a responsible participant in government. We feel the need to be aware of the workings of government, provide leadership where called upon, to respond constructively to government programs as they are initiated. We expect to pay our fair share for government services and in every way to be loyal as a corporate citizen of the country which has given us the free enterprise system.

Symbolizing values.

Some businesses select a symbol that evokes core values. At Featherbone, Gus Whalen has the Chinese word for crisis printed on the back of all copies of the corporate creed. The word consists of two Chinese symbols, one for danger, the other for opportunity. Among family members, this simple set of marks is a reminder of the company's long history of creative adaptation, and of the discipline that will be needed to capitalize on the inevitable crises of the future.

Visual messages.

Wall hangings, sculpture, the design of the business's plants and buildings, or even parking-lot rules, can all reinforce values. Displaying patents, service awards or oil paintings of the founders on the wall may symbolize the value placed on creativity, servant leadership or stewardship. Embellishing bulletin boards with employees' family photos or personal messages, rather than just mandatory government postings, may reflect value placed on openness and trust among stakeholders. Marking prized parking-lot spaces "reserved for the employee of the month," rather than saving them for executives, may reflect the value placed on employee development at all levels.

Telling stories.

Telling stories and parables can build the business culture. At Meijer Stores, a big retail chain, stories told by members of the owning family illustrate a core Meijer value: Treating every person with respect and dignity. One Meijer ancestor had "the only barber shop in town that welcomed black people," Fred Meijer, the builder of the chain, recalled in a speech. Later, Mr. Meijer's father always hired the handicapped and minorities in his grocery stores. Now, Meijer carries on that tradition by employing 11,000 mentally and physically challenged people. That particular value has paid off in the business. During the Depression, Mr. Meijer says, the company's store captured 60 percent of the welfare-relief business in its area. Needy customers came to Meijer because they knew that "even though they were poor, they were treated with dignity," Meijer said.

One third-generation owner of a family business, a food company, used a parable to drive home to a newly hired non-family executive the value the family places on stewardship. On the new executive's first day, the family member instructed him, "Look out the window at the parking lot. See all those cars out there? Those are our employees' cars. Every car out there represents a family. You are responsible to each and every one of those families."

Employee training.

At one large retail chain, a family member travels to every employee orientation, store opening and manager-development class and gives a talk about the owning family's history and values. Family members also discuss the advantages of being a privately held company. This demanding policy requires family members to fly all over the country making speeches to the company's thousands of employees. But family members believe the opportunity to transmit values warrants the effort. These traveling emissaries might be called "cultural ambassadors."

Monitoring behavior.

Staying faithful to core values requires a conscious, planned effort in many businesses. It means ensuring that day-to-day decision making and behavior reflect those values. In some family businesses, executives try to make decisions as if their deliberations were being videotaped for future generations as examples of ethical conduct. This acid test fosters hard-headed concern for ethics. Other companies give annual awards for employee behavior that best exemplifies their values.

In a more formal exercise that might be called "a values audit," family owners of one service concern meet annually with top managers and directors of the business to discuss how day-to-day operating decisions have reflected or failed to reflect the business's stated values. The usual talk about financial performance is excluded from this meeting. Managers are asked to give positive examples showing how values made a difference in the business, or negative examples where breaches of company values were identified. In one instance, the group discussed a new policy requiring all employees at one level of the company to abstain from drinking alcohol at lunch, for safety reasons. Meanwhile, employees in sales continued to entertain clients over drinks at lunch. Managers soon realized the policy violated a core value in the business: Treating all employees the same, regardless of their status in the organization. Although it was difficult, managers decided to impose the same no-drinking rule on salespeople, to achieve the cultural integrity that was all-important to this family business. The decision engendered respect among customers and employees alike.

Such "values audits" remind managers that the family's commitment to values is strong. They inspire family members and reinforce their commitment to the values. And they educate independent directors and remind them of their role in overseeing the business's adherence to values.

In an unusual case, another family business calls family members who violate the family's shared principles to account for their behavior to a council of elders. The transgressor is given an opportunity to explain his or her behavior and argue that the principle should be changed, through an agreed-upon process. However, if family elders reject these arguments, the family member is punished. While this process is extreme, it does suggest a dynamic that other families might embrace in a less formal way: Behavior that violates shared values can be actively corrected by engaging the wrongdoer in a dialog and reinforcing the importance of shared values.

An internal venture fund.

One diversified family business promotes the value it places on entrepreneurship by maintaining an internal venture fund. Any employee with a new-business idea can make a proposal for funding.

If it is accepted, the employee receives time off from the job and venture capital to try his or her idea.

Strategic planning.

One business family has laid explicit plans to integrate core family values into strategic planning. This family shares a deep commitment to church and community, contributes heavily to charity and thinks deeply about how spiritual beliefs should affect business conduct. In keeping with that focus on values, the third-generation successor-apparent in this business has created a new strategic-planning model. Unlike the business-school model of corporate success, which puts "increased shareholder value" at the top of the planning pyramid, his family business model places "successful stewardship" at the peak. Two other important family goals, remaining private and achieving a good rate of growth, share the top level of the planning pyramid. Secondary goals are return on investment, productivity and strategy, hallmarks of the conventional business-school plan. In another departure from convention, all components of this successor's strategic planning model rest upon a foundation of "core values." (Please see Exhibit H.)

EXHIBIT H

A Design for Strategic Stewardship

Increased Shareholder Value	Successful Stewardship / Remaining Private / Growth
Revenues / Productivity	Return on Investment / Productivity
Strategy	Strategy/Vision / Core Values

Conventional
Business School
Strategic Planning
Model

A Family Business
Strategic Planning
Model Integrating
Core Values

Under this model, the family places high priority on identifying, tracking and managing "stewardship" performance variables as they affect shareholders, employees, family and community. These variables include employee compensation and benefits compared with industry norms, profit sharing and pension contributions, church and charitable giving, and family employment and leadership. More conventional measures of return on equity, liquidity and dividends are also tracked, of course. All strategic decisions are weighed in light of all these variables.

Memorials.

Some unusual family businesses preserve, transmit and capitalize on values by creating bricks-and-mortar tributes. Johnstons of Elgin, the 200-year-old business in Scotland, has been operated by seven generations of two families since its founding as a woolen mill. This family business brings to life its history as a producer of fine Scottish woolens in a museum that shares it with the public. Mill tours, an audio-visual presentation available in six languages, and exhibits that show how Johnstons buys, processes and sells its products, all demonstrate its steadfast commitment to the highest quality materials and craftsmanship. The family's values are evident everywhere, from the museum coffee shop to the restrooms in which are displayed the regional tourism board's award for "Best Loo." The mill and museum attract tour buses and sightseers from all over the world. It's a powerful marketing tool: Every visitor passes through a beautiful display of Johnstons' merchandise for sale.

VI. Reinterpreting and Renewing Values in a Changing World

The pace of change in business and the economy has never been faster. New-product life cycles have shrunk dramatically. Companies merge and restructure almost overnight. Industries combine, transform themselves and re-emerge with a different focus. Business strategies are rendered obsolete in a heartbeat.

It is easy in this environment to confuse constants and variables. **Too much change leads to rootless floundering. Too little change leads to irrelevance and death at the hands of the competition. Changing what should remain constant leads to trouble. Failing to change what must bend with the times leads to trouble.**

This chapter discusses how business leaders can remain true to core values, while at the same time reinterpreting and revitalizing them to endure in changing times. Successors play a central role in ensuring values remain flexible but strong. Also, successor generations sometimes face the need to overhaul a legacy of flawed values — principles that may have been compelling for the founder, but that bear the seeds of conflict or serious business problems in the future.

The need for flexibility.

Values must be relevant to changing circumstances in both the business and the family. A retail chain that thrived in the 1940s by stressing hands-on, detail-oriented customer service may be unable to compete today, when saddled with the high labor costs that entails. Customer service may have to be redefined to mean, say, speedier delivery or a faster-changing array of goods.

Owners of Opus Corp., a family-owned developer that has received national industry honors for the quality of its operations, say its success has depended on its capacity to change just about everything — except its values.

> *Too much change leads to rootless floundering. Too little change leads to irrelevance and death at the hands of the competition. Changing what should remain constant leads to trouble. Failing to change what must bend with the times leads to trouble.*

61

Opus rode the changing tides in real estate by continually restructuring its 25-state operations, the *Minneapolis Star Tribune* reported. At one point, it halved its development square footage from previous peak levels, to respond to reduced demand for upscale office space. The firm sharply reduced its inventory of buildings right before a late-1980s commercial real estate crash. It downsized staff by nearly 20 percent. It restructured itself into three regional developers, based in the Midwest, Southeast and Southwest, to respond more nimbly to regional economic change. And it formed an investment arm to buy, develop and re-sell properties.

Through all this change, founder Gerald Rauenhorst and his three adult children who work in the business have maintained Opus's core values of fine craftsmanship, teamwork and integrity. The *Star Tribune's* Sally Apgar wrote, "In an industry that isn't best known for clean dealings and moral integrity, Rauenhorst seems like a priest in developer's clothing. Competitors and insiders say that he and his company live by their integrity and strong value system." These values have enabled Opus, which means "creative work," to retain loyal customers and a sense of direction through restructurings and succession planning.

Coping with change in the family.

Time can place tremendous stress on core values in families too. The succession of business-owning generations can force families to expand the definition of "shared values." First and second cousins' values diverge. Spouses and partners come from different upbringings. As the family umbrella widens, many families are hard-pressed to recognize, much less adhere to, shared values.

Many families find a solution in continuing to stress the fundamentals, but becoming more flexible on the details. For instance, families that adhere to a shared faith may be challenged by an heir's marriage to someone outside that faith. The answer may be in reinterpreting that value: Is it more important that we are Methodists, or that we trust in God? One family faced a question about whether a family member's longtime homosexual partner had the right to be included in family meetings. After hard discussions that tested fundamental values, this family decided that commitment, rather than sexual orientation, was what really mattered. The partner was allowed in.

Other families wrestle with what "commitment to the family" really means. Many entrepreneurs seek to pass on a strong work ethic to their children. Working 80-hour weeks enabled them to build a successful business and support the family financially in fine style.

But members of the next generation may have an entirely different view. To them, an 80-hour week may signify over-commitment to the business at the expense of the quality of family life. In one case, a successor in such a situation made a commitment

Conflicts over values demand a probing re-examination of the beliefs that underlie them. Open, honest communication, genuine effort and an emphasis on the factors that unite the family and the business are essential.

with his spouse to shared parenting and work-life balance. The founder, frustrated and confused, demanded of his son, "You have to make a choice here. Are you committed to the business or not?"

The successor replied, "Dad, you always said you worked so hard so we could have a better life. I want my kids to have a better life too, and one of the ways is that they have a father present in their lives. I understand the cost of the sacrifices you made. And I'm going to continue the tradition of giving our children a better life." What matters most? The shared commitment to "a better life for the family?" Or the founder's commitment to doing personally whatever it takes to make the business succeed? Again, this evolution of values across generations can severely test families' ability to find common ground.

Reinterpreting positive values.

Conflicts over values demand a probing re-examination of the beliefs that underlie them. Open, honest communication, genuine effort and an emphasis on the factors that unite the family and the business are essential.

Many families find a solution through a change in emphasis rather than substance. In one family food business, the second generation began the process of articulating values. The siblings who led the business at that stage embraced stewardship as a shared value. Family members basically trusted them to lead the company. But it fell to the third generation, leading a vastly expanded business, to go beyond loyalty and unexamined trust. Noting major changes in both the business and the family, these cousins openly promoted many of the same shared values, but added a new emphasis: Accountability. Business leaders began sharing certain financial information so the family could assess their progress toward stated goals. Loyalty was still important. Trusting family managers was still important. But the new value placed on accountability helped ensure the flexibility and resiliency needed to endure as a family-owned enterprise.

Fixing a flawed legacy.

In other cases, families in business together need to change the values on which the business has been built. The founder may have passed on values that served the business in the first or second generations, but fail as a foundation for the long run.

The value system may have inherent conflicts. This often happens when a strong founder builds the business on a cult of personality. While the founder's power and charisma may have masked the conflicts and enabled the organization to scrape by, these contradictions get messy when the founder is gone. The founder may have espoused a long-term view, for instance, but refused to plan for succession based on a conflicting value of self-reliance in children. Or the founder may have espoused "taking care of our people" as a paternalistic euphemism for a belief in secrecy as a management tool. Secrecy may be necessary to a struggling startup; if employees knew how hard the founder had to work to make payroll, they might all quit. But as the business grows, secrecy can conflict with "taking care of our people." If you really believe in taking care of people and bringing out the best in them, you have to empower them by giving them information. A failure to share strategic plans, to rally employees around business goals or to articulate thoughtful human resource policies can foster resentment, confusion, directionlessness and a sense that management is unfair. Thus conflicting values give rise to an inconsistent culture.

Conflicting values also can weaken the ownership base of a family business. A family business may value stewardship, for instance, a principle that stresses building the business for future generations. But the same business may grant stock to nonfamily managers who have a proprietary focus on maximizing returns to themselves. Satisfying both sets of owners over the long term can be nearly impossible. Attaining consistency in values is essential. Successors who inherit a culture of conflicting values have a real job on their hands, one that may require a long, hard effort at values education and planning.

Even more troublesome are negative values that undermine business or family success. Powerful, charismatic leadership is required in these cases. One second-generation CEO inherited the reins of a nationwide business from a founder who believed that no one can be trusted. He placed extraordinary value on protecting oneself from a hostile world at all costs. His extreme fear of legal liability led him to balkanize the business into separate corporations divided by legal firewalls. This fostered a culture of individual accountability. However, the dark side was an attitude of "everyone for himself" and "protect your own interests at all costs." This culture made teamwork impossible. It also fostered costly redundancies in accounting systems and administration.

Rather than waiting for crises or disagreements, many successful family businesses make planning for renewal a regular discipline. Leaders of the family, the business or both may meet each year to review a written statement of values.

The second-generation CEO of this business wanted to build trust, teamwork and synergy. In a powerful symbolic move, he managed to get actual pieces of the Berlin Wall after it was torn down, to give to every employee as a sign that a new era of working together would begin under his leadership. He handed the chunks out during a speech on developing teamwork and trust as a way of reaching business goals. He vaccinated the business legally by other means. This CEO's awareness of the importance of values, culture and symbolism as an emblem of it, made him a stronger leader.

Planning for renewal.

Rather than waiting for crises or disagreements, many successful family businesses make planning for renewal a regular discipline. Leaders of the family, the business or both may meet each year to review a written statement of values. Does it need updating? Is it flexible enough to adapt to changing times? If such planning is not done annually, it should definitely occur at key transitions such as succession, or whenever a fundamental question about the direction of the business is raised.

Such efforts can build remarkably strong foundations. Conventional wisdom holds, for instance, that going public has a killing effect on a family business's culture. But rigorous planning has helped Owens & Minor, a medical and surgical supply wholesaler, sustain core values. Since its founding in 1882, Owens & Minor has remained "mindful of our heritage" while staying "focused clearly on today and tomorrow," says G. Gilmer Minor III, a fourth-generation family leader of the business. That heritage includes values that are "an integral part of our culture": A standard of excellence, integrity, caring about people, loyalty, customer service and a strong work ethic.

Family and non-family managers through the years have renewed and transformed Owens & Minor in response to a changing environment, holding all the while to core values. After going public in 1971, the company kept a reputation for integrity in its dealings, for being a loyal business partner, and for fostering a caring environment that helps employees deliver quality service. The resulting close ties with customers paid off especially in the 1980s, when soaring health costs wiped out weaker competitors. By listening closely to customers, Owens & Minor's employees helped them cut costs on products and supplies. The company also developed electronic order placement to help customers reduce inventories and improve product tracking and invoicing. The result was a tenfold sales expansion by 1991.

That expansion posed a new challenge. Faced with a need to reinterpret values to suit the present, Owens & Minor found "some rather sophisticated means to keep the vision alive," Mr. Minor says. The company sent managers on a retreat to reappraise its mission. They emerged with a renewed statement of purpose that echoed the company's longstanding principles. Also, the company continually reminds employees, "sales have expanded exponentially and technology has surged, but the values remain the same." In a symbolic move, it uses an inverted pyramid as an organization chart, underscoring two core values: Customer service and caring about people. Performance and responsibility begin at the front lines, with the employees who come in contact with customers. From there, the goal-setting process filters *down* to the president and CEO, Owens & Minor says. In Owens & Minor's case, a strong value system has clearly been a competitive advantage.

VII. *Summary*

A commitment to values and values education is the most important contribution a family can make to the success of both the family and the business.

A culture based on strong, positive values benefits the family business in many ways. It guides decision making in crises, inspires top performance and motivates employees by lending meaning to their work. Values can fortify strategic planning by encouraging business leaders to challenge conventional thinking and adapt nimbly to change. A strong culture can burnish the reputation of the business in the marketplace, making it more alluring to business partners and employees alike. Values also can strengthen shareholders' commitment to long-term goals by providing a vision that transcends short-term financial goals.

Values play a special role in uniting family and business. When the goals of the family and the business diverge, as they invariably do at some point, shared values can lend a sense of mission and purpose that transcends those conflicts. When values in the business and the family reinforce each other, powerful synergies can arise that strengthen people's performance in both realms.

Values must have certain qualities to work this way. They must be authentic, simple and durable, that is, resilient and malleable to changing times. And they should encompass as many dimensions of family and business behavior as possible. Among twenty winning values we have seen at work in successful business families are accountability, ethical conduct, meritocracy, risk-taking, self-reliance, servant leadership, social purpose, stewardship, valuing stakeholders and fun.

Values are nurtured in the family in many ways. Parents begin early, by setting an example for their children and exposing them to activities and institutions that will reinforce values. In larger, more mature families, a senior family member or any interested person can take the initiative in values education. Families use a variety of processes to identify and agree upon shared values, and many formalize them in written statements. To ensure that values endure, families use such techniques as storytelling, fireside chats, family meetings or seminars.

Building values in the business can begin with a founder, a spouse, a successor or any interested family shareholder. The discussion often starts when questions about leadership or ownership succession arise. A corporate creed or mission statement is a useful communication tool. Some family businesses make values an important part of employee orientation and training. Others set up procedures to track whether values are being followed in day-to-day operations. Still others make use of symbols, memorials and ceremonies to fortify values in the business.

Over time, values must be continually re-examined and re-interpreted to stay relevant amid rapid change in the marketplace and the family. Sometimes this requires a mere change in emphasis. Other times, successors must transform the values upon which the business has been built. These efforts often spark constructive, thoughtful planning initiatives that can yield major long-term benefits to the business and the family alike.

Appendix

EXAMPLES OF FAMILY VALUES STATEMENTS

Example one:

FAMILY VALUES STATEMENT

Mutual respect, honesty and integrity are basic elements of our family and business relationships. Without these, we cannot achieve our *vision* and *mission.*

FAITH
We believe in living a faith-filled life that follows the loving example of Jesus Christ.

FAMILY
We are deeply committed to promoting and perpetuating the unity of our family.

PHILANTHROPY
We support and encourage philanthropy with both time and treasure.

INDIVIDUALITY
We respect and celebrate the special purpose, uniqueness, and freedom of each individual spirit.

COMMUNITY
We will be good, law-abiding citizens to our community and country. We support the perpetuation of the free-enterprise system.

PRODUCTIVITY
We value a strong, pro-active work ethic for a fulfilling life.

EDUCATION
We believe knowledge and education empowers individuals to grow and achieve their dreams.

Example two:

FAMILY MISSION AND VALUES STATEMENT

To plant the seeds of excellence and to perpetuate a commitment to family which fosters love, trust, respect and honor.

As a family, we strive to:

- Act with integrity

- Promote self-esteem

- Teach "sense of family"

- Pursue the love of work

- Cherish individuality, independent thinking, freedom of choice

- Encourage the participation and empowerment of every family member

- Commit to communication and the resolution of conflicts

- Serve as responsible "role models" of productive and creative people

- Create wealth responsibly and confront the challenges of wealth

- Acknowledge excellence as a personal expression, with freedom to learn from mistakes

- Demonstrate pro-active compassion and generosity

- Focus energy on the enhancement of our community

- Create an environment for lifelong learning.

All these to pass on and teach from generation to generation.

Index

74

The Authors

Craig E. Aronoff and John L. Ward have long been recognized as leaders in the family business field. Founding principals of the **Family Business Consulting Group**^{SM}, they work with thousands of family businesses around the world. Recipients of the Family Firm Institute's Beckhard Award for outstanding contributions to family business practice, they have spoken to family business audiences on every continent. Their books include *Family Business Sourcebook II* and the three-volume series, *The Future of Private Enterprise.*

Craig E. Aronoff, Ph.D., holds the Dinos Eminent Scholar Chair of Private Enterprise and is professor of management at Kennesaw State University (Atlanta). He founded and directs the university's Cox Family Enterprise Center. The center focuses on education and research for family businesses, and its programs have been emulated by more than 100 universities worldwide. In addition to his under-graduate degree from Northwestern University and Masters from the University of Pennsylvania, he holds a Ph.D. in organizational communication from the University of Texas.

John L. Ward, Ph.D., is Clinical Professor of Family Enterprises at Northwestern University's Kellogg Graduate School of Management. He is a regular visiting lecturer at two European business schools. He has also previously been associate dean of Loyola University Chicago's Graduate School of Business, and a senior associate with Strategic Planning Institute (PIMS Program) in Cambridge, Massachusetts. A graduate of Northwestern University (B.A.) and Stanford Graduate School of Business (M.B.A. and Ph.D.), his *Keeping the Family Business Healthy* and *Creating Effective Boards for Private Enterprises* are leading books in the family business field.

The best information resources for business-owning families and their advisors

The Family Business Leadership Series
Concise guides dealing with the most pressing challenges and significant opportunities confronting family businesses.

Comprehensive — Readable — Thoroughly Practical

- *Family Business Succession: The Final Test of Greatness*
- *Family Meetings: How to Build a Stronger Family and a Stronger Business*
- *Another Kind of Hero: Preparing Successors for Leadership*
- *How Families Work Together*
- *Family Business Compensation*
- *How to Choose & Use Advisors: Getting the Best Professional Family Business Advice*
- *Financing Transitions: Managing Capital and Liquidity in the Family Business*
- *Family Business Governance: Maximizing Family and Business Potential*
- *Preparing Your Family Business for Strategic Change*
- *Making Sibling Teams Work: The Next Generation*
- *Developing Family Business Policies: Your Guide to the Future*
- *More Than Family: Non-Family Executives in the Family Business*
- *Make Change Your Family Business Tradition*
- *Family Business Ownership: How To Be An Effective Shareholder*

The Family Business ADVISOR Monthly Newsletter

Family Business Sourcebook II

Edited by Drs. Aronoff and Ward with Dr. Joseph H. Astrachan, *Family Business Sourcebook II* contains the best thoughts, advice, experience and insights on the subject of family business. Virtually all of the best-known experts in the field are represented.

Now Available:
John Ward's Groundbreaking Family Business Classics
- *Keeping The Family Business Healthy*
- *Creating Effective Boards for Private Enterprises*

For more information:
Family Enterprise Publishers℠, P.O. Box 4356, Marietta, GA 30061
Tel: 800-551-0633 or 770-425-6673, www.efamilybusiness.com